Where the Blood Mixes

WHERE THE BLOOD MIXES

Kevin Loring

Talonbooks

Talonbooks
278 East First Avenue, Vancouver, British Columbia, Canada V5T 1A6
www.talonbooks.com

Eighth printing: September 2018

Typeset in Minion
Printed and bound in Canada on 100% post-consumer recycled paper

Cover design by Adam Swica

Talonbooks gratefully acknowledges the financial support of the Canada Council for the Arts, the Government of Canada through the Canada Book Fund, and the Province of British Columbia through the British Columbia Arts Council and the Book Publishing Tax Credit.

Library and Archives Canada Cataloguing in Publication
Loring, Kevin, 1974–
    Where the blood mixes / Kevin Loring.
A play.
ISBN 978-0-88922-608-1
    1. Indians of North America—British Columbia—Drama.
I. Title.
PS8623.O74W44 2009   C812'.6   C2008-906200-0

To Jade

Acknowledgements

It takes an army to bring a play to the stage. The playwright would like to acknowledge the artful militia who helped make this one the success it has been. Many thanks to the following people and organizations for their support and inspiration:

Margo Kane, Glynis Leyshon, Marie Clements, Sharon Pollock, John Lazarus, Jovanni Sy, Rachel Ditor, Ken Cameron, Jody-Kay Marklew, Carl Stromquist, Stuart Pierre, Bronwyn Bowlby, Jason Burnstick, Gary Farmer, Kathryn Shaw, Tantoo Cardinal, Rob Lewis, Chelsea McPeake, Meredith Elliott, David Ross, Ben Cardinal, Quelemia Sparrow, Itai Urdal, Carol Chrisjohn, Lori Marchand, David McNally, the Lytton First Nation, Chief Byron Spinks, Raymond Philips, the Canada Council for the Arts, Studio 58, Freda Loring and Guy Neufeld, Floyd Adams, the British Columbia Arts Council, Arts Partners for Creative Development, Luminato, Toronto's Festival of Arts and Creativity, Magnetic North Theatre Festival, Don Shipley, Tom McBeath, Joy Coghill, the City of Vancouver, urban ink, the Kay Meek Centre, Spirit of BC Arts Fund, the Hamber Foundation and the Playhouse Theatre Company.

Where the Blood Mixes premiered June 7, 2008, at the Factory Theatre, as part of Luminato, Toronto's Festival of Arts and Creativity, with the following cast and crew:

MOOCH	Ben Cardinal
JUNE	Margo Kane
FLOYD	Billy Merasty
GEORGE	Tom McBeath
CHRISTINE	Quelemia Sparrow
MUSICIAN / COMPOSER	Jason Burnstick
Director	Glynis Leyshon
Set Design	Robert Lewis
Costume Design	Patricia Smith
Lighting Design	Itai Erdal
Visual Design	Carl Stromquist
Projection Design	Jamie Nesbitt
Stage Manager	Carol Chrisjohn
Apprentice Stage Manager	Bronwyn Bowlby
Technical Director	Kelvin Bonneau

Characters

FLOYD	a native man, middle-age
MOOCH	a native man, middle-age
JUNE	a native woman, middle-age
CHRISTINE	Floyd's daughter, twenties
GEORGE	a Caucasian man, bartender, middle-age
CHORUS	the voices of the children lost in the system
MUSICIAN	

oolh shkeeyAydn quequshtAyp ta.sh pan"t woo.Aya wa
TLK emchEEn whee.Kt zogw"z0gw't tash nahdeep ta.sh
wOOmahh. quequshchAmwh.

[O salmon, thank you for returning to Lytton
(*Kumsheen*), we will be strong now that you have
given us your life. Thank you.]

- Periods (.) represent glottal stops within a word.
- Upper case vowels are enunciated more fully than lower case vowels. For example, if you break the word *shkeeyAydn,* which means salmon, into its syllables, *shkeey–Aydn,* the emphasis in the pronunciation is on *Ay.*
- The *ee* of *shkeey* is the same as in English (as in *seed*).
- When two vowels appear together, it means the vowel sound is extended, as in *shkeeyAydn* and *wOOmahh.*
- This doubling and the differing emphasis between upper and lower case letters are indicators of the tonal qualities of the language.
- The *0* in *zogw"z0gw't* is a fuller *o* sound that is articulated in the middle of the soft palate.
- Upper case consonants denote hard consonant sounds. The double *hh* in *wOOmahh* indicates an extended *h* sound.
- The *OO* in *wOOmahh* is pronounced as an open *oh.* The double vowel is held twice a long as a single vowel.
- In *TLK emchEEn,* the word for Lytton, or *Kumsheen,* the letters *TLK* are, in fact, sounded together as though they are one consonant.

- One of the difficulties that English speakers encounter with our language is that many of its sounds are articulated further back in the soft and hard palates, rather than at the front of the mouth as in English. Also, the relationship between consonants and vowels is quite strange to an English speaker. It is important, therefore, to sound out, as best as possible, the words as they appear, bearing in mind that trying to articulate them with the front of your mouth and lips alone will prove difficult.

- When a fluent speaker speaks the language, it flows together quite beautifully, and has an almost song-like quality that rises and falls in tone, as indicated by the emphasis on the upper case, extended vowels, which are broken by glottal stops and consonants. The words should flow easily into each other. This quality is quite difficult to achieve at first, but with practice the sounds of the language start to make sense.

- It is important to remember that this language has only recently been transcribed into a written form; there have been many attempts, and revisions, to accurately describe these sounds using symbols and letters that are, in fact, quite alien to this very complex language.

Enter young native woman wearing a simple white dress.

The sound of wind blowing across hollow pipes.

A song, a soft and distant lullaby.

Underwater light pours down, diffused by the river's surface. Projected onto the woman is a pictograph, revealed in the shimmering light. She radiates a ghostly aura.

CHRISTINE

I was born in the heart.

I was born in the deepest part.

In the middle of it all, I was born.

In the place where the rhythm beats,

Deep inside my mother,

Where the rivers meet,

My father dreamt me there.

Where blood mixes with blood and the sturgeon waits,

And the wind sings the songs of the dead.

The lights come up and CHRISTINE is gone. FLOYD is in the bar.

The wind blows. The salmon swim away. GEORGE and the bar are blown into the space by the wind. The wind fades away. A guitar plays.

GEORGE
(*cleaning the table*) Hey, Floyd!

FLOYD
Huh?

GEORGE

Go home if you want to sleep.

You were moaning.

FLOYD

Oh?

GEORGE

Uh-huh.

FLOYD

I was dreaming …

> *A pull-tab machine is illuminated up-centre. Its blue and red lights make it sparkle like a giant fishing lure. FLOYD goes over to the pull-tab dispenser, buys a handful of pull-tabs, returns to his table and proceeds to pull them open.*

FLOYD

Hey, were you singing?

GEORGE

Well, since my baby left me,

Du-duh!

I found a new place to dwell!

Du-duh!

The only hole I'd never leave

The Lytton Hotel

Da-doop-ee-doobie

Da-doop-ee-doobie-Du duh!!!

> *Beat.*

FLOYD

Jeezus Christ.

GEORGE

Any luck there?

FLOYD

No. (*pulls one open*)

Nope. No luck here. (*another*)

Nothing.

Three beavers would be nice, eh. Five hundred bucks.

FLOYD pulls open his last pull tab.

Hey—three fish. I got three fish.

GEORGE
Two bucks.

FLOYD hands over his pull-tab to GEORGE.

FLOYD
Three fish —two bucks, then.

GEORGE
You can put it towards your tab.

Beat.

FLOYD
Oh ... Okay.

How much is my tab?

GEORGE
About three beavers ...

MOOCH enters.

FLOYD
I don't remember it being that much.

MOOCH
Hey there, partner.

GEORGE
I added it up.

MOOCH
How's it going?

FLOYD
When?

GEORGE
Just now, I added it up.

FLOYD
Sneaky bugger adds up my tab while I'm not looking.

MOOCH sits and stares at FLOYD.
FLOYD notices that MOOCH looks beat-up.

FLOYD
What the hell happened to your face?

MOOCH
I forgot to put the toilet seat down.

GEORGE
What?

MOOCH
June's miserable, worse than usual, I can't do nothing right.

FLOYD
You never could.

MOOCH
Anyways, I forgot to put the toilet seat down and ... well ... she
went pee in the middle of the night ...

FLOYD
So.

MOOCH
I guess she fell in.

GEORGE
What?

MOOCH
Yeah. She fell right in the bowl. Her cheeks touched water and
everything.
Anyways, she falls in the toilet and she just loses it.
She's screaming and hollering, kicking the walls.

FLOYD
    No shit.

MOOCH
    When I woke up she was right on top of me.
    Woke me up and lumped me out!
    Damn near knocked my tooth out too.

GEORGE
    Holy shit, Mooch.

FLOYD
    Did you hit her back?

MOOCH
    I wouldn't do that.

GEORGE
    You *couldn't* do that. June's twice the man you are. You're lucky to
    be alive.

MOOCH
    Ahhhhh … she's just a little crabby is all.

FLOYD
    Seems like she's always a little crabby these days.

GEORGE
    Ever since she quit …

MOOCH
    Naaaaw, that's not it … It used to be you had to watch your ass
    when she got her moon time, eh, but once that was done, she'd be
    just like an angel.

GEORGE
    (*snickers*) Angel of Death maybe …

MOOCH
    For a couple of days, anyways … But now … now she's got that …
    moon-a-pause.

GEORGE
    Moon-a-pause?

MOOCH

There's no telling what she'll do.

Get a jug.

FLOYD

You gonna chip in?

> *MOOCH reaches into his pockets and pulls out a handful of change.*

FLOYD

How much is that?

MOOCH

Twenty bucks, looks like.

FLOYD

How did you get that?

GEORGE

Raid June's change jar again?

MOOCH

No!

FLOYD

The one she puts money in, instead of buying smokes.

MOOCH

She gave it to me.

FLOYD

You ripped her off!

MOOCH

No!

GEORGE

No wonder she's so miserable all the time. She was trying to save up for something nice and you go and drink it away on her. One day you might find yourself out on your ass.

MOOCH

You gonna lecture me all goddamn night?

FLOYD
How much he got?

GEORGE
About ten bucks, looks like.

MOOCH
Told you. Now c'mon, let's chip in and get a jug. We can get more that way.

FLOYD
I got a drink.

MOOCH
Oh …

MOOCH watches for FLOYD to drink his beer.

FLOYD
You just gonna sit there and watch me?

MOOCH
I'm waiting for you. Hurry up, eh.

FLOYD
Get your own jug!

MOOCH
If we chip in, it's better. C'mon!

FLOYD tries to take a drink. MOOCH stares at him the whole time.

FLOYD
Oh, for Christ sakes!

MOOCH
George, get us a jug.

MOOCH collects his change from the table.

MOOCH
I'll keep this for the next one.

FLOYD
I thought you said you would pitch in.

MOOCH

I'll pitch in for the next one. You get this one.

FLOYD mutters to himself under his breath.

MOOCH

You know, I might look licked, but you really look like shit.

FLOYD

And what the hell are you, a goddamn underwear model?

MOOCH

No, I'm serious; you're more miserable-looking than usual. George, don't you think he looks more miserable than usual.

GEORGE

Let's look. Oh yeah.

MOOCH

Are you on your moon time too? 'Cause you know, men get their moon time too, eh. It's whatcha call it ... whore-moan-all, ain't that right, George?

GEORGE

Oh yeah. Me, I get my period and everything. Bleed right out my arsehole.

FLOYD

Bullshit—that's your piles bleeding!

GEORGE

I get rank too; stink like a bull elk in full rut.

MOOCH

Like right now?

GEORGE

Worse.

MOOCH

Nice!

GEORGE

We gonna go hunting this year, Floyd?

FLOYD

Hunting? With you? You might blow my goddamn head off.

GEORGE

C'mon, me and Mooch went last year. Mooch got that little two-point, isn't that right, Mooch.

FLOYD

You went hunting with this crazy *Shum'ma*?

MOOCH

Him? Oh yeah. We hunted.

FLOYD grunts.

MOOCH

We went up the lake there just road hunting, eh. We're going around the far end there and I tell him, "STOP! Right there! Right there!"

MOOCH points to an imaginary deer.

MOOCH

He hits the brakes, my goddamn head almost went through the windshield.

He indicates antlers with his hands.

MOOCH

Two-point buck right on the road at Dead Lake, there. So we jump out, I lean up on the truck, eh. Crazy *Shum'ma* jumps right in front of me. BOOM!

I almost took his goddamn head off.

FLOYD

That's why I don't want to hunt with you. You get that buck fever.

GEORGE

Ah bullshit.

FLOYD

You get so worked up you forget yourself. Your heart thumps in your chest, you can't hear nothing, your asshole puckers up, your pecker gets hard and your eyeballs pop right out of your head; all because of that an-drenaline, eh, rushing through your veins, and all you can think about is shooting that buck. And then next thing you know—

MOOCH

Somebody's goddamn head is blown off.

FLOYD

(*reinforcing*) Somebody's goddamn head is blown off.

GEORGE

I guess that's a no, eh?

MOOCH

You're one to talk. You almost blew my head off that one time.

FLOYD

When?

MOOCH

That one time up High Mountain there …

FLOYD

That wasn't buck fever … you ducked.

MOOCH

Hey, remember that time we were out road hunting and drinking all day, you picked a fight with … what's his name … he's dead now … anyways, you got licked, remember?

FLOYD

No.

MOOCH

C'mon, you remember.

FLOYD

I'm supposed remember some time I got licked by some dead guy while I was drunk, sometime in the long-ago past. What the hell kind of a question is that?

MOOCH

You know! That time we were on a bender and you passed out on the table there, all bloodied up.

GEORGE brings the pitcher over.

GEORGE
Oh, well that narrows it down.

MOOCH
Remember?

FLOYD
No.

MOOCH
Well I guess not. You were passed out on the bar.

FLOYD
Jeez-us Mooch, what's your point?

MOOCH
Who took care of you? Who?

FLOYD
Ah Christ, here we go.

MOOCH
I did. You know why? Because we're partners! I drug you outside
so George could clean up the mess you made. In-it, George?! I
even put you in a safe place so no one would roll you.

FLOYD
Where?

MOOCH
Anything for my buddies …

FLOYD
Where did you put me?

MOOCH
I was looking out for you.

FLOYD
Oh, you were looking out for me?

MOOCH
Uh-huh.

FLOYD

While you were looking out for me, where did you put me?

MOOCH

Out back, between them garbage bins out back there.

FLOYD

You put me in between some fucking garbage bins?

MOOCH

Yeah, they're covered over so you wouldn't get wet if it rained.

FLOYD

Asshole. Gimme that jug—you don't get nothing!

MOOCH

What did I do?

GEORGE

Just settle down.

MOOCH

What did I do?

GEORGE

Don't provoke him, Mooch. He looks like he's having a bad day.

FLOYD

Why don't you two mind your own goddamn business for once! A guy can't even have a drink without everybody climbing up his ass.

GEORGE

Alright, alright.

FLOYD

I'm sick and tired of it. Sick and tired of you … you … bumming off me. For once, just once, I'd like you to buy me a beer, without me even having to ask.

MOOCH

What for?

FLOYD

Just because.

MOOCH
I'm chipping in—

FLOYD
Sure, you're chipping in with June's money. And when I order another one you'll say, "Oh, I'll get the next one." Maybe. That woman works hard to look after you and all you do is steal from her. No wonder she's always lumping you out.

MOOCH
That's none of your goddamn business.

FLOYD
Oh, is that right, eh. None of my goddamn business ... See? You don't like it, do you. Don't like it when someone looks at you, sees your shit and tells you it stinks. Do you?

MOOCH
I's just being friendly.

FLOYD
Friendly?! You're not my goddamn friend, you're my goddamn Mooch!

MOOCH
Yeah, I'm your Mooch! We're partners.

FLOYD
Well then, partner, how about you buy ME a beer.

　　　Pause.

MOOCH
I'll chip in for the next one.

FLOYD
(*howls*) Hah! That's what I thought.

　　　FLOYD goes back to his drink while MOOCH sits and sulks. Trying to change the subject, GEORGE indicates a newspaper article he's been reading.

GEORGE
Hey, did you hear this thing about people getting compensated?

Pause.

MOOCH
Prune juice works good.

GEORGE
No. People are getting *compensated.* I guess the government and the church are finally going to compensate people for what happened at those residential schools.

FLOYD
Yeah, yeah … it depends on how bad it was, eh. Most people are getting about fifteen grand. If it was real bad, you get lots more.

MOOCH
Goddamn *Shum'mas.*

GEORGE
Hey, I'm a *Shum'ma.*

MOOCH
So?

GEORGE
I never did nothing to you. Don't blame me for what happened.

MOOCH
Are you the church?

GEORGE
No.

MOOCH
Are you the government?

GEORGE
No.

MOOCH
Then shut up. I don't blame you. You're a good *Shum'ma.*

FLOYD
You know why I blame the *Shum'mas?* Because the *Shum'mas* run everything! The Indians, the fishing, the country, the whole world! And every year the whole world gets worse.

GEORGE

Oh, piss off. Don't blame me.

FLOYD

The whole world goes to shit and the *Shum'ma* says, "Don't blame
me!"

GEORGE

Hey, I'm in the same hole as you. I just pour the beers.

FLOYD

Uh-huh. You might pour our beers, and this jackass might take
you hunting, but you're still in charge of us here. In-it, Mooch?

GEORGE

Ah bullshit. I ain't in charge of nothing.

FLOYD

Yeah, bullshit is right.

GEORGE

And what are you doing, Floyd? Sittin' here all day saving the
world one beer at a time!

FLOYD

If the *Shum'mas* let the Indians run the Indians in the first place,
we wouldn't be having this conversation.

GEORGE

Another one?

FLOYD

Yeah.

GEORGE

Anyways … it looks like you're going to get a settlement.

FLOYD

Most of the people that went to that school are dead now
anyways! What good does a settlement do them?

GEORGE

You know, maybe you should run for Chief! Hey, Mooch? Chief Floyd?!

He bitches like a chief.

FLOYD

Goddamn rights! I'd turn this place around!

GEORGE

Oh yeah, you'd turn it around alright, right on its ass.

FLOYD

Bullshit.

GEORGE

You boys will be rich. You could even pay off your bar tab.

FLOYD

Yeah, I'll probably get a couple grand out of it.

But Mooch, there … he had it pretty bad, eh.

Hell yeah, Mooch, you'll be loaded. You could pay me back for the thousands of beers I bought you over the years.

GEORGE

If it was real bad …

But you gotta talk about it, though. That's the thing, eh? You gotta talk about what happened.

FLOYD and GEORGE stare at MOOCH who begins to feverishly open his pull-tabs.

MOOCH

What the fuck are you looking at?

GEORGE retreats back behind his bar. FLOYD just stares at MOOCH.

GEORGE

So …

I guess …

Fishing's opening up, eh.

FLOYD
  Yeah, yeah, I'll probably go down the river tomorrow.

  Silence.

FLOYD
  Hey, Mooch? Wanna beer?

  Transition: The wind blows MOOCH and GEORGE off-stage. FLOYD stands down-centre looking out, above and behind him up centre CHRISTINE is silhouetted.

  All around her, hundreds of crumpled letters float in the water. From the letters come the overlapping voices of the Chorus of the Lost—the disconnected voices of children trying to connect to their families. Salmon flicker in and out of the darkness, with flashes of silver and red.

CHORUS
  Attention. Attention.

CHRISTINE
  To whom it may concern—

CHORUS
  To whom it may concern—

CHRISTINE
  Dear Minister—

CHORUS
  Ministry of—

CHRISTINE
  Family—

CHORUS
  Ministry of—

CHRISTINE
  Health—

CHORUS
  Ministry of My Life—

CHRISTINE
I am looking—

CHORUS
Searching—

CHRISTINE
For my family—
I was—

CHORUS
Abandoned—taken—adopted—

CHRISTINE
My foster parents adopted me. Please help me find my—

CHORUS
People—

CHRISTINE
I have been—

CHORUS & CHRISTINE
Searching—

CHRISTINE
All my life—

CHORUS
Searching—

CHRISTINE
I've always felt—

CHORUS
Disconnected—

CHRISTINE
I've always felt—

CHORUS
Emptiness in my heart—

CHRISTINE
I need to know—
I need to—

CHORUS
Connect—

CHRISTINE
Do I have any brothers, sisters?

CHORUS
Questions—

CHRISTINE
I have these—

CHORUS
Questions—

CHORUS & CHRISTINE
Where are you? Why did you give me away?

CHRISTINE
Who am I?

> *CHRISTINE's special fades and she is gone.*
> *The letters fall to the ground as FLOYD picks up a single letter and begins to read it.*
> *Transition: Pictograph salmon appear and then vanish.*
> *FLOYD is at his fishing spot on the riverbank. Sitting on his stump, with his fishing rod is in his hands, FLOYD is fishing as MOOCH enters.*

MOOCH
Hey there …

FLOYD
Huh? Oh.

MOOCH
You said you were going fishing.

FLOYD
You have to fish here? This is my spot.

MOOCH
You don't own the river.

FLOYD
I showed you this spot.

MOOCH
So.

They stare at each other for a beat.

FLOYD
Arm wrestle?

MOOCH
What?

FLOYD
Arm wrestle for it! I win, you get the hell out of here. You win, you can stay. Come on, you were a logger. You think you still got it in you, or what?

MOOCH flexes one of his biceps.

MOOCH
You want a piece of this?

FLOYD
Come on.

MOOCH
You want a piece of this?!

FLOYD
Maybe you're chicken shit?

MOOCH
I'm not chicken shit!

FLOYD
Alright then! Let's go!

MOOCH
If I win, I get your spot!

FLOYD
Deal! I win and you don't fish here for the rest of the season!

MOOCH
Bullshit! The rest of the season?

FLOYD
C'mon, chicken shit!

MOOCH
I'm not chicken shit!

FLOYD and MOOCH place their elbows on one of the stumps and lock wrists.

FLOYD
Ready, set.
GO!

FLOYD wins the first match.

MOOCH
You cheated!

FLOYD
No I didn't!

MOOCH
Best of three!

FLOYD
Alright then!

They lock wrists again.

FLOYD
Let's get it on! Ready—

MOOCH
WAIT!!
You said it last time! My turn now!
Ready …… Set … GO!

MOOCH wins the second match, but just barely.

MOOCH
(*triumphant*) Whooooooooooo!

FLOYD
Ah bullshit!

MOOCH
Do or die now!

They lock wrists for a third time.

FLOYD
Ready. Set … GO!

It's a back and forth battle until:

MOOCH
OVER THE TOP!

MOOCH changes his wrist position so that his fingers curl over FLOYDs fist giving him the "Over-the-top" advantage. MOOCH is victorious!

I win! I am the winner!

FLOYD
You cheated!

MOOCH
I won! I won, goddamn it! I won!

FLOYD
You cheated!

MOOCH
No way. You got licked. Admit it. Admit it!

FLOYD
Whatever.

MOOCH
C'mon, say it!

FLOYD
What?

MOOCH
Say it!

FLOYD
You …

MOOCH
Say it …

FLOYD
Alright!
You won.

MOOCH
You're goddamn rights I did. Look at this.

He flexes his biceps again.

Look at it. That's logging! Twenty years of packing a chainsaw all
over the countryside. Right there, boy! Right there! Ow.

FLOYD
What's the matter?

MOOCH
Ow!

FLOYD
What?!

MOOCH
Cramp! Cramp! My arm! Shit! My arm! Ow!!!!

FLOYD
Stretch it out! C'mon, stretch it out!

MOOCH
I can't!

FLOYD
Stretch it!

MOOCH
I CAN'T!!

FLOYD massages MOOCH's arm.

MOOCH
Ow. Ow. Oh. Oh.

FLOYD
Better?

MOOCH
Oh yeah, oh yeah, that's better. Oh that feels good. Oh … much
better.

> They look at each other. FLOYD recoils from stroking
> MOOCH's arm.

MOOCH
Well, guess we know who's tougher now, eh.

FLOYD
Ah bullshit.

MOOCH
Should have been a logger instead of a railroader, maybe you'd be
tough like me.

FLOYD
Huh, yeah right. I got a pension; what the hell you got—a bad
back. In-it?

MOOCH
I got your fishing spot is what I got.

> MOOCH sets up his gear in FLOYD's spot. FLOYD is
> not happy as he moves to the less advantageous fishing
> spot. Once he sets up, he tosses his line in and they sit.
>
> FLOYD reaches into his fishing bag and pulls out a
> sandwich and starts eating. MOOCH reacts like a big
> ol' brown bear sniffing the wind.

MOOCH
Jeez, that looks good.

FLOYD
Mmm-hmm.

MOOCH
That salmon?

FLOYD
Mmm-hmm.

MOOCH
With celery and onions?

FLOYD
And pickles …

MOOCH
Jeez, that looks good.

    Beat.

MOOCH
Any more?

    Pause.

    *FLOYD stares at MOOCH. Reluctantly FLOYD gets a
    sandwich out of his bag and tosses it to MOOCH.
    FLOYD also pulls out a beer, cracks it open and starts to
    drink.*

MOOCH
Beer?

FLOYD
Yup.

MOOCH
Sure am dry.

FLOYD
Oh yeah.

MOOCH
Pretty hot today, eh.

FLOYD
Yup, hot one.

MOOCH
Got another one?

FLOYD
Huh?

MOOCH
Got another beer there, Floyd?

FLOYD
What?

MOOCH
C'mon. Don't be cheap.

FLOYD
Jeez-us …

> FLOYD grumbles to himself, but begrudgingly reaches
> into his packsack and tosses MOOCH a beer.

MOOCH
Right on, partner!
Biting?

FLOYD
Just the suckers.

MOOCH
Suckers, huh.
Ugly little buggers …
I tried to eat one once when I was real starving one time. Choked on a bone.
Damn near puked my guts out. Tastes like shit.

FLOYD
Bottom feeders.

MOOCH
Yeah … Bottom feeders.
Hey, what about sturgeon though?

FLOYD
Huh?

MOOCH

They're bottom feeders too, in-it?

Sturgeon tastes good.

FLOYD reels his line in, checks his bait and recasts.

FLOYD

In the summer when the salmon are running, the sturgeons eat the ones that die and sink to the bottom. In the spring they taste better. They're cleaner in the spring, I figure. Can't eat 'em now, anyways. Pollution I guess.

MOOCH

My grandfather used to say that they swam in the river between here and the spirit world.

FLOYD

Whatever the hell that means.

MOOCH

When I was a kid I used to stay with my grandparents in the summers down at Siska, there. I remember this one time fishing for sturgeon with my papa. He used to call me his *Shinge*.

The first day we went down the beach, there. And he had these great big chunks of ham that he used for bait, and he used these great big hooks, and he had them all in a row—about four or five of them—couple feet apart, like, on a rope not even fishing line, and then he had that long rope tied to a barrel for a float, eh. He tied that rope around a tree and threw the baited hooks into the current. We left it overnight. The next day we checked it, and that barrel was floating around in the eddy. Every once in a while it would bob up and down; something big was pulling it down. That sturgeon was dragging it around the eddy. Every once in a while the sturgeon would try to take off down river. WHACK!! That rope would crack tight. My papa knew what he was doing. That fish was caught. We left it caught like that for three days, to tire it out. On the fourth day we went down to the river to go get that fish.

So my grandfather, eh, he brings his horse. And hooks it up to the rope and he gives me a .22. He gives me that gun and he tells me:

"*Shinge!* Go stand on that rock over there by the water. You gonna shoot that sturgeon in the head when it come out. It might kill us when it starts flopping around on the beach."

And I says, "No way, no fish is gonna kill me."

So he gets that horse pulling. And that great big fish starts fighting. That old horse is pulling and struggling against that fish. That must have gone on for hours, eh. Then suddenly it came up, it rolled out there in the river on the surface about thirty feet from shore. It was huge. Like a sea monster! All I saw was fins, foaming white water, then it was gone, back down under the river.

My grandfather hollers, "Get ready!"

So I get up on that rock and I load my gun and my grandfather starts whipping that poor old horse and she starts pulling on that fish, and that great big fish's head starts coming out of the water, and I tell you I never seen anything like it. It must have been a sixteen-footer. It could have eaten that horse! It looked like a dinosaur! Like a great big boney grey crocodile-looking dinosaur fish! And it was pissed! And it was looking right at me. We were eye to eye! And my grandfather yells, "*Shinge!* SHOOT IT IN THE HEAD! SHOOT IT IN THE HEAD!"

FLOYD
So what did you do?

MOOCH
I dropped that gun and got the fuck out of there.

FLOYD
What?

MOOCH
I thought it was going to eat me!

FLOYD
So what happened, what did your grandfather do?

MOOCH
Well, he got it on shore, but it started kicking and rolling around. It got wrapped up in the rope, the horse was going nuts, and by the time he got the gun to shoot that sturgeon, it rolled back into

the river and was taking that horse with it. So my grandfather had to cut the line before the horse got drug under.

FLOYD
Holy shit, it got away?

MOOCH
Yup, it got away. My papa didn't speak to me for a month. Then one day we were out in his garden, I'll never forget, picking beans, and he just starts laughing. He laughed and laughed for about twenty minutes, seems like. Then he looked at me, great big grin, and he says, "*Shinge*, you make good bait."

> *MOOCH reels his line in and recasts.*
> *A train blows its horn a ways down the canyon, the sound echoing up toward them.*
> *Silence.*

FLOYD
My kid wants to come home.

I got a letter. She wants to come home.

I haven't seen her since …

MOOCH
Since she got took? That's a long time.

FLOYD
Yeah, long time.

> *Beat.*

MOOCH
Holy shit.

FLOYD
Yeah. Holy shit.

MOOCH
Well, that's good.

FLOYD
I don't even know what she looks like …

What if … what if she doesn't like me?

MOOCH
Well, why would she?

FLOYD
What?

MOOCH
No offence, partner, but you're not the most likeable guy.

FLOYD
Who asked you?

MOOCH
All I'm saying is. You need to work on being more …
more … pleasant-like.

FLOYD
Pleasant?

MOOCH
Yeah. Pleasant. You're an owl-y son of a bitch. You don't want to
scare her away.

FLOYD
No. I don't want to do that.

MOOCH
You should practise.

FLOYD
Practise?

MOOCH
Yeah, you could practise on me.

FLOYD
Bullshit!

MOOCH
If you could be nice to me, you could be nice to anyone.

FLOYD
You got a point there …

They sit for a bit as the giant sturgeon overhead swims effortlessly in the eddy.

FLOYD hooks the sturgeon above the stage. The giant fish fights the hook.

FLOYD
  Holy shit!

FLOYD dives for his fishing rod.

FLOYD
  Got one!

MOOCH
  Reel it in!

FLOYD fights with his fish.

FLOYD
  It's a big one. Get the net! Get the net!

FLOYD fights the fish back and forth along the riverbank.

MOOCH
  Play it out!

FLOYD
  Too big to be salmon!

MOOCH
  It's a sturgeon.

FLOYD
  I'm not ready!

MOOCH
  Hold on!

FLOYD
  I'm not ready!

FLOYD struggles with the massive fish.

MOOCH
  Don't let her go!

41

FLOYD
I … can't … hold … it!

The line snaps.

FLOYD
Goddamn it! I wasn't ready!

MOOCH
Holy shit!

FLOYD
I told you!
Should have had the net ready!

MOOCH
Rushed it—

FLOYD
I never could have landed it anyways, too big, too much to handle.

MOOCH
Uh-huh.

FLOYD
Next time, next time I'll be ready.

MOOCH exits.

FLOYD stares into the river. The sturgeon swims down stream.

Transition: The silhouette of a small child appears in a doorway.

CHRISTINE
Daddy, daddy, I can't sleep.

FLOYD
Christine?

CHRISTINE
I had a bad dream.

FLOYD
What were you dreaming?

CHRISTINE
I don't know.

FLOYD
It's just a dream. Go back to bed.

CHRISTINE
How do you know?

FLOYD
Because. I know. Now go back to bed.

CHRISTINE
Daddy?

FLOYD
What?

CHRISTINE
A woman came to school today.

FLOYD
Oh yeah.

CHRISTINE
She asked me about you.

FLOYD
A woman? What did she want?

CHRISTINE
I don't know. She smelled bad. She smelled like … like … like stink.

FLOYD
She smelled like stink?

CHRISTINE
Uh-huh.

FLOYD
What did she want?

CHRISTINE
She wanted to eat my bones like in the dream. Like the *Neeshta*. She wanted to get me. She wanted to take me away.

FLOYD
Why would she want to do that?

CHRISTINE
She thinks you're bad.

FLOYD
How do you know she thinks I'm bad? What did she say?

CHRISTINE
She said I needed a bath. She said I looked hungry.

FLOYD
Didn't you make yourself a lunch? I told you to make a lunch.

CHRISTINE
I did.

FLOYD
What did you make?

CHRISTINE
Chocolate bar.

FLOYD
And?

CHRISTINE
I don't know …

FLOYD
You don't know?

CHRISTINE
Gummi bears.

FLOYD
That's it?

CHRISTINE
Jujubes.

FLOYD
    You had a chocolate bar, gummi bears and jujubes for lunch?
    I thought I gave you money for lunch.

CHRISTINE
    Uh-huh.

FLOYD
    How come you didn't go and get something better?

CHRISTINE
    I don't know.

FLOYD
    Well, next time get something better.

CHRISTINE
    Uh-huh.

FLOYD
    You're not dirty, are you?

CHRISTINE
    I don't know.

FLOYD
    Do you stink?

CHRISTINE
    No. You stink.

FLOYD
    I don't stink.

CHRISTINE
    Uh-huh, you stink like fish … (*She giggles.*)

FLOYD
    I'll show you stink. Now get to bed, you little fart, or the *Neeshta* is
    gonna get you.

CHRISTINE
    Daddy?

FLOYD
What now?

CHRISTINE
My clothes are wet.

FLOYD
How come your clothes are wet?

The silhouette fades out.

FLOYD
Baby? How come your clothes wet?! Christine?!

A phone rings. Lighting shift as FLOYD wakes up and answers it.

FLOYD
Hello? (*beat*) Hello?

Lights up on CHRISTINE, now an adult, at her home in the city.

FLOYD
Hello.

CHRISTINE
Hi. Is this Floyd Couteaux?

FLOYD
Who's this?

CHRISTINE
It's me. It's Christine.

FLOYD
Oh.

CHRISTINE
Did you get my letters?

FLOYD
Uh … yeah. Yeah, I did.

CHRISTINE
Can I see you … ?

Beat.

CHRISTINE
I'd like to meet you.

FLOYD
Yeah. Yeah you can meet me. If you want …

CHRISTINE
Are you sure? If you're not sure, that's okay you know. I'll … I'll understand.

FLOYD
No, no …
I'm sure.

CHRISTINE
Okay. Good.

FLOYD
Okay.

CHRISTINE
I can come … in about a week.

FLOYD
A week?! No.

CHRISTINE
No? Is that too soon?

FLOYD
No. That's good. That's good.

CHRISTINE
You sure?

FLOYD
Yeah.

CHRISTINE
Okay.

FLOYD
Yeah. That's good. That's good.

CHRISTINE's special fades. Transition into bar: FLOYD is moping around. MOOCH is sitting at a table in the bar. A huge pile of opened pull-tabs is in front of him.

MOOCH

(*pulling open pull-tabs*) Beavers, beavers, beavers … Ahhhh, shit, no beavers!

GEORGE

You know what's funny. If you just saved the money you spent on those things, you'd be rich. Instead you spend all your money, or should I say June's money, on those goddamn pull-tabs hoping to win back a little bit of what you spent.

MOOCH

Yeah, but … three beavers is five hundred bucks. And there's how many of those in here. What if I got two in a row? You wouldn't question me then, would you.

GEORGE

Whatever.

MOOCH

Besides, it's not good business for you to dis-encourage me from playing.

GEORGE

Did I dis-encourage you, Mooch?

MOOCH

No.

GEORGE

Then I've got nothing to worry about, do I.

MOOCH

Hey, twenty bucks! See, George. Told you.

C'mon, partner. I'm buyin'. Twenty bucks, partner.

Remember how Anna used to call us "partners in crime and hard times"? Remember?

Come on! I'm buyin'!

GEORGE
    Beer, Floyd?

MOOCH
    Get him a beer.

FLOYD
    Well, alright. Twist my rubber arm, why don't you.

        MOOCH proudly pays for the beer.
        JUNE enters the bar.

JUNE
    Mooch!

MOOCH
    Oh shit.

JUNE
    Can I speak to you a moment? *Haat-choo-tza!* [Let's go—Now!]

GEORGE
    Oh Jeezus, this is going to be ugly.

        GEORGE and FLOYD watch the big battle.

JUNE
    We sat down last night and I poured my heart and soul out, and
    you sat and listened. And you promised me you wouldn't steal
    from me, but you did, didn't you? DIDN'T YOU?

MOOCH
    I didn't, June Bug! I didn't!

JUNE
    Where did my money go then? Huh? That was for the phone bill,
    that money.

MOOCH
    What money? I don't know what you're talking about.

JUNE
    Don't insult me! I work, Mooch. I work to try and support us.

MOOCH

I know, June Bug, I know.

GEORGE and FLOYD laugh.

JUNE

(*to FLOYD and GEORGE*) SHUT UP!

GEORGE and FLOYD shut up.

MOOCH

I never took nothing from you, June Bug, nothing—

JUNE hits MOOCH. WHACK!!!
GEORGE and FLOYD burst out laughing.

MOOCH

Owww!

JUNE

Don't lie to me! Where's the rest of my money.

MOOCH

I don't know—

JUNE hits MOOCH again. WHACK!

GEORGE

Yup, just like an angel.

FLOYD

I feel better already.

JUNE storms over to GEORGE.

JUNE

If you see him in here again, you call me, you hear.

GEORGE

No, that's stupid; he's a grown man. I'm not going to do that.

JUNE advances menacingly.

JUNE

Useless sons of bitches!

JUNE storms out of the bar.

FLOYD

I'll call you! Don't worry, June! If I see him in here, I'll call you right away!

GEORGE

That's just mean. That's just cold-blooded.

FLOYD raises his glass.

FLOYD

Uh-huh, here's to June Bug, may all her blows land true.

Transition: FLOYD is staggering home. He makes it across the stage and then collapses on the side of the train tracks. Off in the distance a train horn sounds; it's a lonely sound, echoing up the river canyon. He tries to get back on his feet and collapses again. The train sounds its horn again, much closer. He struggles to get back on his feet, but he is too drunk and collapses again. A light shines on him, which gets brighter and brighter. The horn sounds again. This time it is deafening; the train is bearing down on him, but he is too intoxicated to move out of the way fast enough. The sound of the train is right on top of him when, out of the wings, a young native woman emerges carrying a brilliant bundle in her arms, a long white dress trailing behind her. As the sound of the train roars past, she crosses to FLOYD, who, with all his strength, is only able to lift his head to see her. When she reaches him, he accepts the bundle from her. As she leaves him, the bundle begins to unravel between them. There is a tug-of-war. The bundle, now unravelled, is torn from FLOYD and trails behind the woman as she exits down river. The sound of the train fades as it passes in the distance.

Transition: MOOCH is standing on the riverbank. FLOYD is caught between the last image and the present scene with MOOCH.

MOOCH

You ever …

You ever wonder what's down there?

FLOYD
Huh?

MOOCH
Below the surface, like?

FLOYD
Fish, rocks, sand, broken pieces of railroad …

MOOCH
Sometimes … sometimes I have this dream, eh … where I'm underwater, out there, where the rivers meet out there. Where they mix. Way down underneath, there's this house, like. Like an old house with smoke coming out of the roof, like there was a fire in there.

FLOYD
Underwater?

MOOCH
Yeah. There's this old man there. In the house. And when I go down there it's like he was expecting me, he knows my name. He knows all our names and all our old buddies are down there. Sitting around the fire, bullshitting, telling stories. I go over to the fire and they were just carrying on. But they can't see me. It was like I was like a *shni'ee*, like a ghost to them. I want to party with them. But all I could do is watch.

FLOYD
Huh.

MOOCH
You ever think about all those people that fall into the river and never come out. Them ones that don't get found …
You ever wonder what … what happens to them?

FLOYD
They drown, they die, and then they get washed down the river. What's the big mystery?

MOOCH
I don't know about that.

FLOYD

There's no rhyme or reason to it, you know? Don't matter if you're a good person or an asshole. The river doesn't care who you are. It'll take you or it'll just spit you out.

MOOCH

How many people we know got took by the river?

FLOYD

Lots, I guess.

MOOCH

They never found Anna. She never come out.

FLOYD

No, they never did.

MOOCH

Those great big sixteen-footers, that's what's down there.

Cleaning up the ones that drown, the ones that commit.

Eating the dead.

FLOYD

What are you talking about?

MOOCH

Do you think that maybe them big old bastards down there ... you think they ... clean 'em up like that?

FLOYD

Hell, I don't know.

MOOCH

Then we catch 'em and eat 'em. So if someone gets took by the river and their body gets eaten by a sturgeon, and then someone catches it and eats it ... in a way that person gets eaten too. And maybe a part of them gets to go on living inside of us ... you know ... over and over again.

FLOYD

Until what, your next trip to the can?

Jeez-us Christ, Mooch! I come down here to get some peace, not to listen to your crazy bullshit.

A train sounds its horn. The sound makes FLOYD uneasy. He looks up towards the train bridge above the river. FLOYD exits, leaving MOOCH alone staring into the swirling river. Suddenly MOOCH leaps into the swirling current and lands in the bar, just as he's finishing a drink.

MOOCH
Ahhhhh! That hit the spot.

GEORGE
You're going to get me in a lot of trouble with June, you know.

MOOCH
No, you'll be fine.

GEORGE
The other day she threatened me on the street. I don't want no trouble with her, okay?

MOOCH
Don't worry.

Tonight might be my last night on earth, anyways.

GEORGE
What?

MOOCH
June is gonna kill me.

GEORGE
Why?

MOOCH
She is gonna fucking slaughter me.

GEORGE
Now what?

MOOCH
I just drank her grocery money.

GEORGE
What?

MOOCH
I just couldn't help it.

GEORGE
You drank her grocery money?

MOOCH finishes his drink.

MOOCH
Yup.

GEORGE
Holy shit, Mooch.

MOOCH
Yup.

GEORGE
So what the hell are you guys gonna eat?

MOOCH
I don't know. Fish?

GEORGE
Why the hell did you tell me that?

MOOCH
I don't know.
I thought you wouldn't care, anyways.

GEORGE pours a shot.

GEORGE
Well, it was good knowing you.

MOOCH slams the shot down.
FLOYD enters wearing a brand new shirt.

GEORGE
Oh no! Who died?

MOOCH
Ah shit! I never even heard there was a funeral today. Goddamn it!
I never find out until the food's gone!

FLOYD
Nobody died. My kid is coming into town today so I wanted to look good.

MOOCH
You wanted to look good?

FLOYD
Yeah. I wanted to be presentable. She's a city girl. They have … you know, high standards. I didn't want to just look like a bum.

MOOCH & GEORGE
OH.

FLOYD
How do I look?

MOOCH
Kinda like a bum going to a funeral.

FLOYD
Go to hell.

GEORGE
No. You look. You look … sophisticated … eh?

MOOCH
Yeah. Oh yeah. You bet. Hey, you can wear that to my funeral.

FLOYD
Huh?

GEORGE
He just drank June's grocery money.

FLOYD
Holy shit.

GEORGE
Oh yeah. He's toast.

MOOCH
I've been dying my whole goddamn life anyways!

MOOCH stumbles.

FLOYD
Hey, take it easy there, partner!

MOOCH
Come here.

> *MOOCH holds out his hand. They lock hands.*

Remember ... when we were kids ... I do. I remember everything.
I never thought about it lots though, till now.

FLOYD
Ah shit, Mooch. Don't think about that stuff.

MOOCH
I can't stop thinking about it.

FLOYD
George, get Mooch here a beer; he needs a drink.

MOOCH
Hey, can I have five bucks?

FLOYD
What for?

MOOCH
'Cause you're being nice.

> *FLOYD gives MOOCH five bucks. He plugs the*
> *illuminated pull-tab machine.*

MOOCH
I've got to win June some money or she's gonna kill me.

GEORGE
He's pretty licked, still early yet too.

FLOYD
Just never mind. Get him a beer.

> *FLOYD pays for MOOCH's beer.*

MOOCH
Hey, right on, partner—just like I told him, hey. Nice.

MOOCH

Anna was good to me. She was nice. I loved her. I did. I loved her like a sister. She was always good to me.

FLOYD

That was a long time ago.

MOOCH

Don't matter how long ago it was. It happened yesterday, it happened today, it'll happen tomorrow. Every day is every day.

He finishes pulling open his pull-tabs. Nothing.

FLOYD

Now you're talking bullshit again.

MOOCH

You know what was bullshit? All us kids locked up in that school only five minutes from home. I could look out the windows and see the smoke from the chimney of my house. Couldn't run home though, or they'd put my parents in jail, in-it?!

I could never figure out how come it was against the law to see my parents. I used to think I must have done something wrong.

GEORGE brings MOOCH his beer.

FLOYD

I don't want to talk about this. Today is supposed to be a good day.

MOOCH

I used to run. Remember, you never ran. You were scared. Me, I'd hoard all the food I could and then when I had enough, I'd run.

I'd run for the hills. I always got caught though. Someone always turned me in.

One time I ran. I was trying to make it to my papa's. Only made it as far as the bridge though, cops were waiting for me. They caught me right in the middle of the bridge. I had nowhere to go.

I looked down and I thought, *Fuck it. Can't catch me down there …*

But I's chicken shit, eh … couldn't jump, scared. They took me back. That priest was waiting. He wasn't even angry, seemed like.

He put his hand on my shoulder, took me down into the basement. Beat me, starved me. Fucked me.

That was the first time I seen the shadows move like that ... then it's like I seen them everywhere. Sometimes those shadows get right down inside.

FLOYD
Christ you're ugly sometimes.

MOOCH
You started it, you and George!

FLOYD
I don't want to talk about this.

MOOCH
You're sick too. That's why you're such an asshole. Me too. I'm sick of me too.

JUNE
(off-stage) MOOCH!

MOOCH
Oh shit.

GEORGE
Into the can! Into the can!

> MOOCH staggers into the men's washroom just as JUNE enters.

JUNE
Mooch! Get out here right now. Goddamn it!

GEORGE
June, take it easy.

JUNE
Shut your lips. I'll knock you right on your ass!

GEORGE
Okay.

FLOYD
Oh, June. Calm down.

JUNE
Who asked you? Was I talking to you?!

FLOYD
No, but—

JUNE
Then shut up and sit down before I lick you too!

FLOYD sits down.

JUNE
MOOCH!

GEORGE
He's not here.

JUNE
Bullshit! I can smell him!

JUNE looks around the bar suspiciously. She stands in front of the men's room.

JUNE
You better not be in there, BOY! 'Cause if you are, I'm gonna tear you a new asshole!

JUNE notices FLOYD's shirt.

JUNE
Oh no!

FLOYD
What?

JUNE
Who died?

FLOYD
Nobody died! I just … I dressed up is all.

JUNE
You clean up good.

FLOYD
My kid is coming home.

JUNE
What kid?

FLOYD
Anna's kid. Christine.

JUNE
What?

FLOYD
Mooch didn't tell you? I told him a while ago.

JUNE
That son of a bitch never told me anything!
Oh my god that's …

FLOYD
Yeah.

JUNE
That's so awesome! Oh my god, that's awesome. That's so awesome.

JUNE gives FLOYD a great big bear hug.

JUNE
Anna would be happy.

JUNE crushes FLOYD to her chest. MOOCH peeks his head out of the can.

MOOCH
What the hell is this!

JUNE
I thought you weren't here.

MOOCH
I can see that. I can see you thought I wasn't here. I step into the can for one second—

JUNE
What? What are you going to do about it?

CHRISTINE enters the bar.

MOOCH
  Why were you hugging him?!

JUNE
  Are you jealous?

MOOCH
  No!

FLOYD
  We weren't hugging.

MOOCH
  You were; I saw you!

FLOYD
  C'mon. It wasn't like that.

MOOCH
  You were making out!

> *MOOCH shoves FLOYD.*

JUNE
  We were celebrating you, asshole!

MOOCH
  You screw around with my woman behind my back?!

> *MOOCH takes a swing at FLOYD.*

JUNE
  What are you talking about?

FLOYD
  I wasn't making out with June!

> *MOOCH and FLOYD stumble across the bar. They wrestle a bit.*

GEORGE
  Hey you two! Smarten up! You're too old to be acting like this!

FLOYD
  That all you got?!

*JUNE notices CHRISTINE for the first time, standing in
shock at the door. As MOOCH and FLOYD wrestle
awkwardly around the bar, FLOYD's shirt gets ripped.*

FLOYD
My shirt!

JUNE
Stop it!

MOOCH
Come on!

JUNE
Stop it!

Stop!

*The two men lunge at each other as JUNE screams at
FLOYD to stop. FLOYD hits MOOCH and he goes
tumbling to the ground. FLOYD jumps on top of him
but GEORGE grabs hold of him and starts to drag him
outside. FLOYD shrugs him off.*

GEORGE
That's it! You're both barred out! Now get out of here before I call
the cops!

*FLOYD sees CHRISTINE for the first time. She doesn't
know who he is. FLOYD recognizes her immediately. He
storms out of the bar.*

*Transition: CHRISTINE enters the bar space. JUNE is
sitting at the bar, GEORGE is behind it. CHRISTINE
goes over to the pull-tab machine. She plugs it with
some money, receives one ticket from the machine, then
pulls it open.*

CHRISTINE
What does three beavers mean?

GEORGE
Bullshit! How many tickets did you buy?

CHRISTINE
One.

GEORGE
You got three beavers on the one and only ticket you pulled?

CHRISTINE
I guess? What does that mean? Did I win?

GEORGE
Did you win?

JUNE
You hit the jackpot! Five hundred bucks!

CHRISTINE
Really?

GEORGE
Let's see. Yup, three goddamn beavers. Hey, you want a beer to celebrate?

JUNE approaches CHRISTINE.

CHRISTINE
I'll just have a ginger ale.

GEORGE
Ginger ale?

JUNE
Get her a goddamn ginger ale and shut your pie-hole already. Christ sakes!

I'm June.

CHRISTINE
Christine.

JUNE
Can I join you?

CHRISTINE
Uh … okay, sure.

JUNE
Where you from?

CHRISTINE
The city. Actually, I'm from here. I mean. I was born here. I can't believe … I can't believe I just saw that. That was … pretty … hardcore.

JUNE
It can be like that around here sometimes.

CHRISTINE
Those two old guys fighting like that? Whoa.

JUNE
So … what do you do in the city?

CHRISTINE
Oh, I'm an artist. Or at least I'm trying to be an artist. I do spoken word and stuff.

JUNE
Spoken word? You speak words?

CHRISTINE
Uh, poetry, and I paint and draw … that kind of stuff. I'm going to art school.

JUNE
You're an artist. That's awesome.

CHRISTINE
Yeah.

JUNE
That's so awesome.

CHRISTINE
Yeah.

JUNE
So what are you doing here?

CHRISTINE
I'm looking for something … someone … actually.

JUNE
Uh-huh.

CHRISTINE
I was supposed to meet him here, but for all I know he's the guy that just got his ass kicked.

JUNE
Oh … no, that wasn't him. The guy that got beat up was my boyfriend.

CHRISTINE
Oh no. I'm sorry.

JUNE
NA! He deserved it.

CHRISTINE
Oh. Okay.

Uh, were they fighting over you?

JUNE
No. Not the way you think, anyways.

CHRISTINE
Um … I have a picture of him … my dad, maybe you know him. He was a lot younger when that was taken …

CHRISTINE shows JUNE her picture of FLOYD.
GEORGE brings over her ginger ale.

JUNE
Look at that.

JUNE shows GEORGE the picture of FLOYD.

GEORGE
That's you?

CHRISTINE
Yeah.

GEORGE
That's Floyd?

JUNE
Look how young he was.

GEORGE
Doesn't look anything like him now, eh ...

JUNE gives GEORGE the stink eye, warning him to get away. GEORGE goes back to the bar.

JUNE
You look just like her, you know. You look just like your mom.

CHRISTINE
I do?

JUNE
I knew who you were the moment you walked in here.

CHRISTINE
You did?

JUNE
Your mom and I were close. I knew her real well.

CHRISTINE
Really?

JUNE
Oh yeah. We went through a lot of times together. We grew up together, eh, her and I. I was there when you were born.

CHRISTINE
You were?

JUNE
Oh yeah. I was there. Shit, I was there when you were made! Well, in the next room, anyways. You look just like her. You really do. You really do.

CHRISTINE
What ... what was she like? My mother.

JUNE
Oh, Anna was beautiful, thick long hair. She was ... she was sensitive, you know ... everybody picked on Mooch, but for some reason she always felt sorry for him.

CHRISTINE
Mooch?

JUNE
My boyfriend, the guy—

CHRISTINE
—that just go this ass kicked? My mother and him were friends?

JUNE
Yeah, I got soft on him too, over the years; that's how we got together. He can be sweet, you know.

CHRISTINE
Oh yeah?

JUNE
That's how he sucks you in.

CHRISTINE
So … my mother?

JUNE
Oh, your mother … She and I liked playing basketball, eh. We'd play in tournaments and all that … when we were young. You wouldn't know it from looking at me now. I could run like the wind. Your mother too. We would run all over the countryside, chasing boys.

They laugh.

JUNE
When she fell in love with your dad, that was it—she was head over heels.

Try to talk sense to her. No way. Your dad … He was a real stud in them days. Everybody wanted a piece of him. We would go to parties and some chick would try and pick a fight with your mom, because they liked him or whatever … They were jealous, eh.

But I'd knock them flat on their asses, boy!

Anna was my best friend.

CHRISTINE
I wish I could have known her.

JUNE

Yeah.

CHRISTINE

The only thing I was ever told was that she died.

I don't even have a picture of her.

JUNE

She was so happy when you were born.

Maybe we should go find your dad, eh?

CHRISTINE

Okay. Oh my god! I can't believe I'm finally going to meet him.

I have, like, these real old memories of him, but I can't remember his face, you know. It's more like a feeling. A smell.

GEORGE

I know that smell. I smell him all the time.

JUNE

Shut up, George.

CHRISTINE

I haven't seen him since … I don't know what to expect. I just want to put a face to the feeling, you know?

JUNE

Maybe I should go get him … let him know you're here.

CHRISTINE

You think?

JUNE

Yeah, maybe that would be best, eh?

CHRISTINE

Oh, okay.

> *JUNE exits.*

GEORGE

Here you go: five hundred bucks.

> *Fade out.*

Outside.

JUNE is walking to FLOYD's house. She runs into MOOCH sitting on the curb.

MOOCH
What were you doing with him?

JUNE
What is wrong with you?

MOOCH
Were you trying to get back at me?

JUNE
You know I don't have much. I don't have a lot to give. I feed you. What am I supposed to buy groceries with now?

MOOCH
When my settlement comes in—

JUNE
I don't want that money!

MOOCH
Well, what then?!

JUNE
I'm so tired of this. You said you would never steal from me after the last time, and all the other times you took from me.

MOOCH
C'mon, June.

JUNE
I can't keep giving to an empty hole. Every day I wonder, *What will he do now?* Every day I am disappointed. Every day I have to act like a crazy person to get you to even think about doing right by me. What the hell is that worth?

MOOCH
June.

JUNE
You break my heart.

MOOCH
C'mon, June.

JUNE
I'm done.

She pushes him away.

JUNE
I can't give you anymore. I'm done.

MOOCH
June Bug.

JUNE
What the hell am I worth to you? A jug? A case, maybe—is that all I'm worth to you?

MOOCH
Come on.

JUNE
Fuck you, Mooch. Fuck you.

She exits.
He reaches into his pockets and pulls out a pull-tab. He opens it. Nothing. Drops it on the ground. He laughs. The laugh fades and he is quiet, alone.
CHRISTINE enters. MOOCH looks up at her. She tries to ignore him.

MOOCH
Anna?!

CHRISTINE
No. I'm Christine.

MOOCH
Come here a minute.

CHRISTINE
I, uh—

MOOCH
Come here!

CHRISTINE
I have to go.

He reaches out to her and grabs her arm as she tries to pass.

MOOCH
Come here, goddamn it!

CHRISTINE
Let go of my arm.

MOOCH
I didn't know you were going to get hurt.

CHRISTINE
What?

MOOCH
I couldn't help it!

CHRISTINE
What are you talking about? Let go of me.

MOOCH pulls her closer.

MOOCH
No! I won't let you go!

CHRISTINE
Let go of my fucking arm!

CHRISTINE pulls free of MOOCH.
She backs away from him and exits. MOOCH stands alone.
Fade out. Transition into FLOYD's house.
FLOYD is sitting at the table. There is an open bottle of whiskey on the table. There's a knock at his door. He tries to ignore it; another knock.

FLOYD
What?!

Knock.

FLOYD
Who's there?!

Knock.

FLOYD
What do you want?!

JUNE
Floyd?!

FLOYD
What?

JUNE
Floyd, let me in!

FLOYD
What do you want?!

JUNE
Damn it, Floyd, if you don't open this fucking door, I'm gonna break it down!

FLOYD
It's open!

JUNE enters. She just stares at FLOYD from the doorway at first. Then:

JUNE
What are you drinking?

FLOYD
Thought you quit.

JUNE
I am quit.

She sits down across from him, he offers her the bottle. She takes the bottle from him and then pours it out onto the floor.

JUNE
This is for Anna. After all this time she's come home.

FLOYD

Yeah. After all this time Christine's come home and that's the first thing she sees: her old man fighting in the goddamn bar.

JUNE

Well, you two should smarten up! What in hell is the matter with you, anyways, acting like children! Like a couple of goddamn teenagers. Your whole life you guys act like children! I'm sick of it! Aren't you sick of it?

FLOYD

He started it!

JUNE

So!

FLOYD

He started it, not me! I didn't start nothing.

JUNE

Oh shut up.

Silence.

JUNE

She looks just like Anna.

FLOYD

When I saw her there in the bar, I damn near had a heart attack.

JUNE

She's seems smart too. *Un*like her old man, that's for sure.

So what are you going to do?

FLOYD

What do you mean?

JUNE

She came all the way out here just to see your sorry ass. What are you going to do? Just sit here and pout like a goddamn child?

FLOYD

I can't see her now!

74

JUNE
Why?

FLOYD
Look at me! Look at me, June! I'm … I'm … I got nothing,
nothing to give her. Soon as she sees me now, she'll … she'll …

JUNE
What?

FLOYD
SHE'LL NEVER WANT TO SEE ME AGAIN!

JUNE
Ahhhhhh BULLSHIT!

FLOYD
No, you bullshit!

JUNE
You're just scared! You're just chicken shit!

FLOYD
You're goddamn rights I'm scared. I am chicken shit, alright! I've
never been so scared my whole useless goddamn life!

JUNE
But now you've been given a chance. Can't you see that? Can't you
see that you've been given a second chance?

FLOYD
What does she want from me, anyways?!

JUNE
She came all this way without any expectations. She came all this
way with an open heart. To give you … to give us all, maybe … a
second chance …

Are you gonna take that second chance or are you gonna let her go
away again.

Empty-handed.

FLOYD
She probably heard about the settlement money and now she's
come to get a piece!

75

JUNE

That's bullshit and you know it!

There is a knock at the door. They are both startled out of their moment.

CHRISTINE

Hello?

FLOYD

Oh shit.

CHRISTINE stands at the open door. She recognizes him from the bar.

CHRISTINE

It's you … I … found my way here. I just knew where to go. I guess somehow I just … remembered. Can I come in?

FLOYD

No! I don't want to see you!

JUNE

Floyd!

CHRISTINE

But I just want to talk to you—

FLOYD

Go away!

CHRISTINE

You said you wanted me to come here … You said you wanted me to come home. Didn't you?

FLOYD

What do you want from me!

CHRISTINE

You said you wanted to meet me! Were you lying? Why would you do that?

JUNE

Come on, Christine, let's go.

CHRISTINE
WHY WOULD YOU DO THAT TO ME?!

FLOYD
Get out! Get out of my house.

JUNE
Floyd!

FLOYD
GET THE FUCK OUT OF MY HOUSE!

JUNE begins to move CHRISTINE out of the house.

CHRISTINE
I found you. I came looking for you. I came looking for you!

JUNE
Come on. He doesn't deserve you. Let's go.

JUNE and CHRISTINE exit FLOYD's house

CHRISTINE
Oh my god. He doesn't want me. He never wanted me.

FLOYD slumps to the floor down-centre.
Slow fade to …
Montage: "Ashe' Mashe'" is played / sung.
GEORGE mops up the mess of the evening throughout.
A special on CHRISTINE crying lights and fades. A special on JUNE smoking lights and fades. A special on FLOYD sitting down-centre lights and fades. Then a special on MOOCH as he removes his shoes and lifts his head to the light as it brightens and then fades. By now, GEORGE has crossed the stage, mopping as he does so until finally his task is done. He takes a rag from his pocket, wipes the sweat from his brow and, as he looks up, the light fades on him as well.

Transition into the next day: CHRISTINE and JUNE are walking along the singing bridge, the sound of the wind gently blowing over the hollow rails of the bridge.

It's a beautiful sunny day. An osprey is circling
overhead. FLOYD is sitting at the bottom of the river,
down-centre throughout.

JUNE

This place … This place is called *Kumsheen* in our language.

Most people say it means the place where the rivers meet, but an
elder once told me that the real meaning is "*the place inside the*
heart where the blood mixes."

CHRISTINE

It's so beautiful here. The mountains, the rivers … I love how one
river is all brown and dirty and the other is blue-green and clean,
and how they mix and become one. Right here, right at this place,
it's … magical almost.

JUNE

You know, they say that Coyote got his guts split open on that cliff
up the valley, there, when he was fighting a giant; you can see the
different colours in the granite that look like intestines. That's his
guts on the rock, his heart was thrown into the river here. This
place is the heart of our people.

CHRISTINE

Wow. That's gory.

JUNE

That's us. All blood and guts, eh.

CHRISTINE

I looked this place up when I got the file on my parents.

JUNE

Oh?

CHRISTINE

I read that the people used to believe that the land of the living
and the land of the souls were separated by a river, and that they
were connected by a slippery log. And when you died, if your
spirit made it across the log, you would be in the land of the souls
and you would never need or want anything forever …

JUNE

And what happens if you don't make it across …

CHRISTINE

Well, the book said that if you fell off the slippery log into the river, your soul would just disappear.

Silence.

JUNE

I want you to have this. (*She removes her necklace.*) It was your mother's. She gave it to me a long time ago. You should have it now.

She puts it around CHRISTINE's neck.

CHRISTINE

Thank you.

JUNE

No, not thank you, *Kookstum.*

CHRISTINE

Kookstum.

JUNE

Kookstcheen, you're welcome. So what are you going to do?

CHRISTINE

Oh … don't worry about me. I just need to … forget this place. I mean … he wasn't in my life before, right? I survived. I just have to put this behind me. Get on with my life. I just wanted to meet him, you know? I thought it would be different.

JUNE

Yeah.

CHRISTINE

Well now I know, don't I?

He wasn't worth the effort.

CHRISTINE turns to go.

JUNE

When your mother died, I think it was like your dad died too. You could just see it in his eyes, he was never the same. People were scared of him. People were worried about you … And so they took you and they never gave you back.

I should have taken you in.

CHRISTINE

It's okay.

JUNE

No, it's not okay! It's not okay, goddamn it! I should have tried harder. She was my best friend. I should have taken you both in. Before she …

JUNE regains her composure.
Silence.

JUNE

It's like a sickness, really, this community is still sick from it after all these years, it never goes away, just tries to get deeper and deeper inside us. It's invisible, eh … this sickness in our hearts. It's just a thought, really, a thought that makes us sick. It was someone else's thought that was taught to us. It's like they were so afraid of us that they had to teach us to be smaller than them … and we learned it real good. Our kids are sick with it too. They got it from us. The drinking, the drugs, the violence, they learned it from us. When you look at it, when you really look at it, that's where it comes from; it comes from us and we came from that school.

We were all there: your dad, your mother, Mooch—us kids, we were all there together.

I tried to forget. I tried so hard to bury it, eh. I didn't know why I was fighting all the time, why I was drinking my face off, why I hated myself. It was just normal to me.

Then one summer … we camped up Pasulko … the lake up in the valley, there. I was having a smoke and the sun was just starting to set. You could see the cotton from the cottonwood trees floating in the air. I was watching the fish jumping in the lake. It must have been the light on the water. I remembered camping up there with my grandmother when I was a little girl. She always smelled like wildflowers. I remembered sitting with her under a cottonwood tree. She was combing my hair, and she was singing this lullaby to me. And then all these other memories started to surface, almost like … like the fish jumping.

And then it was like my guts were ripped open and all the pain came back to the surface, all the hurt was raw again, only worse. I fell to the ground right there, and I thought I would never get up. I cried and I cried until I couldn't cry anymore, until my eyes were dry. I cried until the stars came out. When I got back to the camp, everybody was already hammered. But, I couldn't join them. I sat there and watched the fire burn down until it was just embers. I just couldn't bring myself to have another drink.

> *Silence.*

JUNE

Oh look, you can see the fish. You can see the salmon down there in the eddy.

CHRISTINE

Oh yeah.

JUNE

oolh shkeeyAydn quequshtAyp ta.sh pan"t woo.Aya wa TLK emchEEn whee.Kt zogw"z0gw't tash nahdeep ta.sh wOOmahh. quequshchAmwh.

[O salmon, thank you for returning to Lytton (*Kumsheen*), we will be strong now that you have given us your life. Thank you.]

That's my quickie fish prayer. Too bad I didn't have a pull-tab prayer too, eh?

> *They laugh.*

JUNE

Your father does love you. He's ashamed of himself. You know? He's carrying a lot of pain, a lot of guilt. He doesn't know how to begin again. People get stuck. Some people get so stuck in it. Sometimes they just need a kick in the ass to get 'em started.

> *The osprey plunges into the water.*
> *Snap transition: CHRISTINE turns to face FLOYD.*

She clutches her necklace for strength. JUNE sits at the edge of the bridge throughout.

CHRISTINE

I don't want anything from you. I have a family, alright. I have people who care about me. Who love me, who loved me when I didn't love myself!

FLOYD

I didn't—

CHRISTINE

Who took me in when I was alone—

FLOYD

I didn't mean to—

CHRISTINE

SHUT UP! Just shut up and listen! I waited my whole life for you to … I came looking for you. I FOUND YOU. And now I'm here. So now you're going to listen to me.

FLOYD

Okay. Okay … come inside.

CHRISTINE enters the doorway.

CHRISTINE

I thought you would be curious about me. I thought that you would want to know what happened to me.

FLOYD

I do.

Silence.

FLOYD

So … your family, they raised you good?

CHRISTINE

They love me. When things were hard, they were there for me.

FLOYD

I always thought about you. I always wondered where they took you. I always wondered where you were.

CHRISTINE

I was moved around a lot at first. There are a couple of years I don't remember at all. I remember being alone, scared. I felt abandoned. Like something was missing, inside. Like something was wrong with me. That maybe that's why you gave me away.

FLOYD

It wasn't like that—

CHRISTINE

Just … let me … I realized that I needed to come home. I needed to meet you. I had to. Even if you never wanted to see me again, I had to come home. I couldn't move forward without knowing where I came from. There was this voice inside me just screaming. And so …

FLOYD

Here you are.

CHRISTINE

Here I am.

CHRISTINE stares at him waiting for a response … but all she gets is silence.

CHRISTINE

Maybe I was wrong.

Maybe I was stupid for coming.

She goes to leave.

FLOYD

No, I'm stupid. I'm the one …

Last night … I …

This is … this is your place too, eh. I mean. This is your house too. There are still scribbles on the wall in your old room. From when you were a baby … you know.

CHRISTINE's childhood drawings illuminate on the set; pictographs shown in previous scenes—a house, fish, people—are projected in collage.

FLOYD

You drew pictures on the wall. I never … I never washed them away. Couldn't, I guess.

For a moment, CHRISTINE enters the pictograph house and becomes part of the images.

FLOYD

At the bar last night—

The pictographs fade.

CHRISTINE

June told me everything. How it started.

FLOYD

June.

CHRISTINE

June is great. I really like her.

FLOYD

I've known June as long as anyone. There was a whole bunch of us, eh, back in the day. Most are gone now.

CHRISTINE

You're a survivor.

FLOYD

We both are, I guess.

CHRISTINE

Why didn't you look for me?

FLOYD

I did. I tried to. They said … that it would be best for you to grow up in a family that could give you more. More than what I could give you.

CHRISTINE

Did you love me?

FLOYD gets defensive …

FLOYD

Of course I did. You were my daughter, you are my daughter, goddamn it! I did the best I could. I just … After your mom died … I had nothing, nothing to give to anyone … You got took. You went into the system and I thought, *That's it.*

CHRISTINE

So you just let me go.

FLOYD

I wish I never did. I wish I never let you go … but—

CHRISTINE

You never fought for me?

FLOYD

What could I do?! The government people said I was unfit.

CHRISTINE

Unfit?

FLOYD

I was fucked up, eh, over your mother; over myself … I couldn't hold onto you. I just couldn't hold on. It was too much, too big for me, by myself.

There was nobody. Just you and me, and I just … I tried but, I couldn't do it.

CHRISTINE

Right.

> *Pause.*

CHRISTINE

How did my mother die?

FLOYD

Your mother … she …

She killed herself. She jumped off the bridge at the end of town there, the one that sings when the wind blows.

> *Silence.*

FLOYD

She had that depression, eh … I mean we all got stuff that … hurts, you know, but she would get so stuck in it. I couldn't do nothing … I got frustrated. I made it worse. I made it hard. I lost my temper on her, eh. She was just so hard to be around, you know? Moody, depressed, crying all the time … I didn't know what the hell was wrong with her … I would get mad at her, or I would just take off, you know, leave her alone with you. There was nothing I could do, anyways … Ah hell, I didn't even try. I was just … ignorant, so fucking ignorant.

I was on a bender with Mooch. I hadn't been home in about a week, just partying; having a good old time. She came into the bar dragging you behind her. She wanted me to come home and I just snapped. I just lost it on her, I was hollering at her in front of everybody, in front of the goddamn bar. Screaming and hollering at her. She didn't say anything. She left you there at the bar and she just … walked away. She just walked away. Mooch took you and went after her. And I just sat there. I just sat there in the goddamn bar. When he came back, he was holding you in his arms. You were both crying.

They never found her … there's a grave … but there's no coffin, even, just a stone, a marker. They never found her body. I blamed him for it, for not stopping her. But … but, it was me … it was always me. It's not your fault what happened. Okay. It's not your fault.

I just let her go. I didn't do anything to stop her. I just let her go. I should have gone after her. I should have done something!

Finally FLOYD breaks down. CHRISTINE hesitates and then slowly reaches out to him and puts her hand on his shoulder. Finally, they embrace.

CHRISTINE

Okay. It's okay. Oh. There's that smell.

FLOYD

Ah Jeez, am I rank? 'Cuz I might be on my man moon time, eh. Men get their moon time too, you know.

CHRISTINE
No. You smell like home.

FLOYD
Ah … I stink like fish.

They laugh in their embrace.

FLOYD
Here.

FLOYD reaches into his wallet and pulls out a picture of he and Anna in a picture booth.

FLOYD
I was going to give this to you last night but … anyways. That's your mom. That's me. And that big lump in her belly is you.

CHRISTINE
Oh my god. I really do look like her.

FLOYD
Yeah, you really do.

CHRISTINE
Do you want to see your grandson?

FLOYD
What?

CHRISTINE
Yeah. Here.

She digs into her purse, then pulls out some pictures and gives them to FLOYD.

FLOYD
Grandson?

CHRISTINE
He's five now. I was pretty young so my parents have been helping me raise him so I could have a life. Finish school. They're really good at spoiling kids, that's for sure.

FLOYD
Is that them? Those *Shum'mas*—I mean white folks, they're your parents?

CHRISTINE
They couldn't have kids of their own. They love him.

I can't wait for you to meet them.

Silence.

CHRISTINE
Oh, I mean you don't have to if you don't want to.

FLOYD
No, no. It's alright. I'd like to meet them … someday.

He's a good looking boy, takes after his mother.

He holds her hand.

FLOYD
Thank you. Thank you for coming home to me. *Kookstum.*

The light of day illuminates the room.

"Ashe' Mashe'" plays again briefly as father and daughter are illuminated in the light of the new day. The song fades into the sound of wind blowing over the hollow pipes of the singing bridge. The light fades on FLOYD and CHRISTINE. MOOCH is standing in the middle of the singing bridge. He is looking over the edge, watching the swirling green water mix with the sandy brown as the two rivers meet. JUNE approaches. She watches MOOCH for a moment and then stands beside him.

JUNE
What are you doing?

MOOCH
Huh? Oh, nothing.

A wind gust makes the bridge sing a little louder.

JUNE
I was worried about you.

MOOCH

What for, I thought you dumped me. Am I still dumped?

JUNE

I don't know, Mooch. I was just worried that you didn't come home last night.

MOOCH

You still mad at me?

JUNE

It's not about me being mad at you.

MOOCH

Anna jumped right here. I was right over there holding … that girl, Christine. I held her, right over there when her mother jumped. I couldn't get to her. I had that little girl in my arms and I couldn't think. All I could do was watch. Anna looked at me, she wasn't even scared. I watched her fall, all the way. All the way down. When she hit she never came up. She was gone. She just disappeared.

JUNE

Yeah, she just disappeared. She left her kid. She gave up. She just disappeared and left all this behind. Well, I'm right here, Mooch. Can you see me?

MOOCH

My name's not Mooch.

JUNE

She's gone, Edgar. You want to go be with her? Then go. I don't care! Go on then! You goddamn jackass. Jump!

MOOCH looks at her for the first time, realizing what she is worried about.
Silence.

MOOCH

I cross this bridge every day.

The wind increases and the low mournful song of the singing bridge strengthens. MOOCH exits, leaving JUNE standing alone looking down at the salmon swimming home, pulled by an overwhelming need to return to the place of their birth. Still further we descend. In the dark light of a deep pool the ancient sturgeon waits, her long sensuous ghost-grey body gently swaying in the current below.

Curtain.

Journey Inside *Where the Blood Mixes*

Beginnings

This play started out as a monologue I wrote in theatre school. Part of the program's graduation requirement was writing and performing a fifteen-minute solo show. Titled *The Ballad of Floyd*, the piece was a portrait of a lonely native man in a bar, celebrating the birthday of his only daughter, whom he had lost to the mean city streets of the city. I performed this piece at the 2001 Talking Stick Cabaret in Vancouver, the precursor to the Talking Stick Festival, an annual aboriginal arts festival held by Margo Kane's Full Circle: First Nations Performance.

It was then that I decided to try and expand the piece into a full-length play. It was my working intention to "let this play teach me how to write and produce a play."

One of the characteristics of the original monologue was that it suggested a continual cycle of alcoholism for the main character. In the first draft of the new one-act version, I played with the idea of the bar being a kind of purgatory for Floyd, and that he kept waking up inside the bar over and over again until he decided to break the cycle by leaving the bar once and for all. This version of the story evolved over several drafts, even garnering some attention by the Factory Theatre's Cross-Currents Festival of New Works, where it received a workshop and a staged reading with veteran native actor Gary Farmer reading the lead role of Floyd. In fact, probably the most important event to come out of that workshop was some feedback I received from Gary on the first day of the workshop.

The cast is sitting around a table.

Enter GARY FARMER, a very large and highly respected native actor. He sits down quietly, smiling and greeting everyone at the table. The VERY YOUNG PLAYWRIGHT nervously shuffles his papers.

DIRECTOR: Shall we get started? Does anybody have any questions, comments before we begin?

The YOUNG PLAYWRIGHT shudders with excitement.

GARY violently slams the script onto the table.

GARY: Thirty-five years in the business and here I am playing another drunken Indian in the bar. So what? So he's a drunk in the bar. So what now?

The YOUNG PLAYWRIGHT pees himself.

That statement struck right to the core of what was wrong with the piece. He was right. So what? After four years of working toward this draft and having a fairly successful workshop and reading in Vancouver, all of sudden somebody finally just said it out loud: So what? What was the greater story I was trying to get at, what was under the alcoholism, under the pain and isolation of this character? Why was he so damaged in the first place? And where could it go from there? For two years I didn't touch the play; I didn't even want to look at it. For two years I thought about, *So what?*

Where the Blood Mixes

Sometime during those two years, I wrote a poem about fishing by the river back home:

Down here
In the shadow of the bridge, the Billy-goat's-gruff-old man-haggardly-troll
sits on the river bank
Rod between his knees,
"Cuzzin," he says, "Come here. Sit with me a while, down here in the shade."
An empty case of beer, a pile of fish heads in the sand
Still eyes bulge in horror at their severed ends,

A bucket of headless silver bodies glisten in the sun
A freshly massacred feast
Wasps and flies hum in ecstasy as the old man sits and smokes.
I sit with him, wondering into spinning pools,
What lies below the fractured surface?
Does the ancient sturgeon wait for us?
A hundred and fifty years long
Her bone-grey body gently caressing the current
Coaxing it to keep her in place,
Hovering in the eddy
Ghost-like, watching, waiting
As the anxious salmon struggle home,
Their passing painted in shadows on the riverbed below.

(I lost the original draft of the poem when my computer crashed. This one is a close approximation.)

In the meantime, I worked as an actor, wrote sporadically for the radio and took on some small stage projects. It was during one of these projects that I met and quickly became friends with Sharon Pollock. At the time, Sharon worked for the Alberta Playwrights' Network and offered to work with me on *The Ballad of Floyd*. This gave me the motivation I needed to tackle the play again. At first I thought I was just going to rework some of the scenes, but as I got into it, I found myself rewriting the entire thing. And to my surprise, the poem about the old man fishing below the bridge, which I thought was lost, resurfaced in the rewrite—becoming in many ways the world of the play. When I finished the draft, it was so unlike the previous version, I decided to rename it: *Where the Blood Mixes*.

The title comes from the translation of the N'lakap'mux place name *Kumsheen,* the location of the village now called Lytton. For years, people have said that this means "the place where the rivers meet" or "meeting place," and to some extent it does, as it is the confluence of the Fraser and Thompson Rivers. However, a more accurate translation would be "the place inside the heart where the blood mixes." This is a reference to *Kumsheen* being the heart of the N'lakap'mux Nation, and it also refers to a story involving the hero Coyote. Coyote was disemboweled along a great cliff in an epic battle with a Transformer, a giant shape-shifting being that could transform the world with his powers. To this day, his intestines can still be seen strewn along the granite walls. In his rage, the Transformer tore Coyote apart and scattered his body across the nation, his heart landing in the place where the rivers meet. Another reason for this meaning is that during the salmon runs, as the salmon are coming up the river, their bodies begin to change to a brilliant blood-red. Back in the days before modern commercial fisheries and habitat destruction, the rivers would be so thick with salmon, it was said you could almost walk across the river on the backs of the fish, the runs were so abundant. It is easy to imagine, then, that this name would quite accurately describe that vital yearly spectacle.

This play is meant to expose the shadows below the surface of a community, and to celebrate its survivors. St. George's Residential School is like a ghost that still haunts my community. When the Lytton Indian Band finally got control of the land it occupied, they tore the old school down, the memories of it too painful, the building itself like a monument to that pain. Now only the old stone church remains. But the memories of that place and time still live on deep inside the hearts of those who spent their childhoods there. And for some, the legacy of that trauma has been passed down through families for generations now. In recent years, the Lytton Indian Band has built its own school and an elder's centre on the grounds where the old red brick institution once stood. The Stein Valley School's curriculum incorporates traditional knowledge and teachings along with the necessary provincial educational requirements. In this way, our people are trying to counteract the damage done by the residential school system to our culture, and to give future generations a sense of pride and self worth—things so vital that were robbed of many of St. George's survivors.

After the 2006 Calgary workshop, as part of my residency at the Vancouver Playhouse, then artistic director Glynis Leyshon directed a staged reading of the play. Immediately afterward, she came to me with a seemingly simple proposition: "Let's get in a van with some actors and take this play to Lytton." So we started applying for grants. Right from the beginning we were awarded some monies and things were looking promising. Then we got a startling request; we were invited to the 2008 Luminato international arts festival in Toronto. For my first professional production, this was quite an opportunity. Shortly thereafter, the piece was also invited to the 2008 Magnetic North Theatre Festival by incoming artistic director Ken Cameron, who had just left the Alberta

Playwrights' Network to take up his new post as head of the roving Canadian theatre festival. He was a fan of the piece, as he had just witnessed the complete transformation of the play in Calgary and was very eager to continue the festival's tradition of supporting new aboriginal works. So all of a sudden the notion of, "Let's get in van and take it to Lytton ... " became, "Let's premiere at a major international arts festival *and* the most important Canadian theatre festival in the same month, on opposite sides of the country!" In the winter of 2008, we did indeed get in a van with a bunch of actors and, in partnership with the Vancouver Playhouse, Western Canada Theatre in Kamloops and Luminato, began a staged workshop development tour. For two weeks, we worked on the piece in Kamloops, with actors on their feet and pages in hand, before embarking on a two-week tour of the play through the BC interior, with limited tech and a live musician. There were performances in Kamloops, Trail, Lytton and, finally, Vancouver, where we had a reading at the Talking Stick Festival. This workshop tour was coupled with readings of *The Ecstasy of Rita Joe* to commemorate the fortieth anniversary of George Ryga's seminal play.

We began rehearsals for our two premieres in May 2008 at the Kay Meek Centre in West Vancouver. This was quite a luxury, as we were able to continue fine-tuning the script with a full set and lighting grid, and could develop the projections and stage the piece in real time. We were also able to preview the play in front of a live audience before we premiered it in Toronto. We continued to fine-tune the script throughout, making structural changes to scenes even after our premiere in Toronto. In fact, on our flight back from a successful three-show run at Luminato, Glynis turned to me fifteen minutes before we were to land in Vancouver and suggested a major rearrangement of Floyd and Christine's reconciliation scene! This was something we accomplished, or more importantly our poor actors accomplished, in time for the western Canadian premiere at Magnetic North, where, like during the Luminato run, we were very well received. All this was taking place at a time when the federal government was conducting the Truth and Reconciliation Commission on the residential school experience in Canada. In fact, on the very day we opened at Magnetic North, the Conservative government officially apologized in the House of Commons for the atrocities committed at the residential schools, and for the legacies that still affect aboriginal Canadians today. It should be noted that our opening date was determined several months in advance of the announcement of the apology. Perhaps it was extraordinary coincidence that the two events occurred on the same day, perhaps it was something more. Either way, the power of that important day resonated deeply with all of us.

However, the most important moment in all of this for me was that sunny day in February at the Memorial Hall on the Reserve in Lytton. Without the benefit of lighting, and having only the bones of a set, with pages in hand, the actors performed this play about my community and the shadows that lurk beneath its surface to the very people I was attempting to portray. I sat behind my uncle Floyd after whom the main character is named. Every time he heard his name mentioned, he couldn't help but giggle behind his hand. The people laughed, the people cried and, in the end, the people cheered. They heard and saw for the first time their own story being told, their own words being spoken. For me, that day wasn't about theatre, it was about something deeper. That day we were family. That day, we were all in the place inside the heart where the blood mixes.